CHOSEN FOR
MORE

JUST AS YOU ARE

Amber Albee Swenson

Published by Straight Talk Books
P.O. Box 301, Milwaukee, WI 53201
800.661.3311 • timeofgrace.org

Printed in the United States of America
ISBN: 978-1-949488-07-4

Contents

Introduction

At a particular point of weariness in my life, I began an intense study of the book of Matthew. Whether you're new to the Scriptures or you've been reading them most of your life, one thing is evident from Matthew chapter 1: Christ's ancestry was as colorful as it gets. His forefathers and foremothers were not of the squeaky-clean variety. There were all kinds of unrighteous people nestled in with the righteous.

Just a few chapters later, Matthew talks about the beginning of Jesus' ministry. This got me thinking about having a calling.

Ephesians 2:10 declares, **"We are God's handiwork, created in Christ Jesus to do good works, which God prepared in advance for us to do."**

These two lessons in Matthew remind me that when it comes to God's kingdom, there's a place for everyone. God's already prepared us to do whatever it is he wants us to do, and nothing except our own excuses and willful disobedience disqualify us from the call. Scripture shows God only needs one person to lead a generation, to free his people from slavery, to rescue the lost, or to take the message where it's never been before.

Whether your sphere of influence is tiny or worldwide is of no consequence to God. He'll use you right where you are in big and mighty or small but purposeful ways.

In this book we'll look at a variety of people from the Bible, the tasks God had for their lives, their flaws or weaknesses, and the outcomes. We'll be reminded God can use anyone. That means he certainly can and will use us.

Grace and peace,

Amber Albee Swenson

Ruth:
Determined to Survive

When I was 21, I participated in a global studies program in college. For months we studied the culture, language, and history of Vietnam before traveling there.

Nothing prepared me for the culture shock of the experience. It began on the flight to Taiwan when, for the first time in my life, I was a minority. That was nothing compared to getting out of the plane at Tan Son Nhat International Airport in Ho Chi Minh City. When we were finally through customs, we stepped outside the airport to an enclosure surrounded by a massive iron gate. We were only allowed to leave when our tour guide arrived. For the next ten days, we depended on him to keep us alive.

The four chapters of the book of Ruth chronicle the life of Naomi, a Jew, and her daughter-in-law Ruth, who was from Moab. Though Moab was just on the other side of the Dead Sea, it might as well have been half a world away. The Moabites had a different language, different culture, and different gods.

Just the word *Moab* likely conjured up shame, resentment, and hatred in some Israelites. There was a history of hate between Israel and Moab dating back to the days of Moses. When God wouldn't allow the false prophet Balaam to curse Israel, the king of Moab and Balaam came up with a Plan B: send Moabite women to seduce the Israelite men by inviting them to partake in Baal worship that involved wine and sex. Many of Israel's leaders fell hook, line, and sinker, and God's wrath wasn't far behind.

With that as the backdrop, imagine Ruth coming to Israel with Naomi. We are continually reminded she is a foreigner and a Moabitess; strike one and strike two against her. The women arrived in Naomi's homeland with nothing: no husbands or means to support themselves—strike three.

Ruth's goal was to stick by her mother-in-law and provide for her. There was just one problem. She was a foreigner and didn't know what she was doing.

When Ruth decided to pick up the leftover grain from the fields, as the poor were allowed to do, we get a hint that she didn't know how it was done in Israel. Boaz, the owner of the field, said to his servants: **"Let her gather among the sheaves and don't reprimand her. Even pull out some stalks for her from the bundles and leave them for her to pick up, and don't rebuke her"** (Ruth 2:15,16).

When did you last feel completely out of your league, up against a wall, unsure how things were supposed to be done? Getting married, starting a new job, stages of parenting, taking care of elderly parents or a sick spouse often bring us to new scenarios that go beyond our prepared-ness. And what about the new things we try in hopes of reaching the

When did you last feel completely out of your league?

world for Christ? Just about the time we think we have things figured out, circumstances change and we're out of our league again. What do we do?

From the start Ruth was determined. Ruth 1:18 says, **"When Naomi realized that Ruth was determined to go with her, she stopped urging her."** Ruth could have determined to make a life for herself and not care about or for her mother-in-law. She could have gone back to the gods of her youth. Instead, she was determined to go with Naomi and stick with the God of Israel.

Ruth reminds me of the woman in Jesus' parable about the widow and the unmerciful judge. As the woman continually came to the judge for help, the judge said, **"Even though I don't fear God or care what people think, yet because this widow keeps bothering me, I will see that she gets justice, so that she won't eventually come and attack me!"** (Luke 18:4,5).

Being determined is far better than my first instinct, which is to retreat and quit altogether.

Years ago friends of ours with children several years older than ours told us their coping mechanism for dealing with teens. They didn't. Each evening the parents locked themselves in their room because they couldn't deal with their children's issues and attitudes.

Now that I have a house full of teens, I understand that desire. But Ruth didn't stop when it wasn't fun anymore. She didn't turn back when Naomi started complaining about being empty. She didn't run back to Naomi when she didn't know how to glean. She hung on and determined to move forward, even if she didn't do it perfectly.

What an example for us! How might things be different if we determined to parent rebellious children, work with our spouse, be the spark at church, and love the grumpy neighbor? Even when we don't do it perfectly, we can strive to be the light in this dark world. When we stumble, we regroup, pray for forgiveness and strength, and then keep going.

Even when we don't do it perfectly, we can strive to be the light in this dark world.

Being determined was not the only attribute that helped Ruth. She also listened to the advice of the godly people around her. Both Boaz and Naomi told Ruth not to go to another field but to stay in Boaz' field to enjoy the protection and provision he would give. Ruth obeyed.

Later when Naomi proposed Ruth go to Boaz to encourage him to consider being her redeemer, Ruth responded, **"I will do whatever you say,"** and we're told that **"she went down to the threshing floor and did everything her mother-in-law told her to do"** (Ruth 3:5,6).

Ruth sought wisdom from the godly people around her. When they told her what to do, that's what she did. We could avoid a lot of trouble if we did the same! I sometimes forget to ask for advice at all. Other times I seek counsel in all the wrong places.

King Solomon was the wisest man to live. When Solomon died, his son became king. He sought advice from older men who served his father. But he also sought the advice of his friends whom he grew up with (1 Kings 12). In the end, he ignored the advice of the older, wiser men and decided to follow what his friends suggested. As a result the kingdom was torn apart.

Philosophies from the popular daytime talk show host or late night comedian are acceptable in the world's eyes. Musicians and YouTubers readily give advice. But are we so eager to go to God's people, the Bible, or to God in prayer?

Solomon said, **"Walk with the wise and become wise, for a companion of fools suffers harm"** (Proverbs 13:20).

God blessed Ruth's determination and obedience. Eventually Boaz and Ruth were married, and Ruth, a Moabitess and foreigner, ended up in the genealogy of Christ.

May God give us the same determination to continue the work he has for us to do and to seek and find solid biblical advice from godly people and our study of the Word. And then, like Ruth, may he give us the strength to carry it out.

More to Think About

1. Often our determination is geared toward the wrong things. We're determined to make money or make a name for ourselves or to be the best at something that has no spiritual significance. What godly goals need to move front and center in your life?

2. If you could get godly advice from anyone, who would it be? Why would you choose this person?

3. Call, email, or meet this person or persons and discuss how you might incorporate your new godly goals. Ask his or her advice concerning steps to take, who to involve, etc., and ask him or her to pray for and encourage you.

Lord God, I so easily fall prey to distraction. Rearrange my priorities to align with your purposes and plans for my life. Give me the determination to carry these out. Help me lead well in love and obedience to you. Please be the loudest voice in my life. In Jesus' name. Amen.

Jeremiah:
The Unappreciated Prophet

In spring 2017, I fell in love with the Old Testament book of Jeremiah. It chronicles the life and ministry of its namesake prophet.

At the beginning of the book, God told Jeremiah that before his birth, even before he was formed in the womb, God knew and appointed Jeremiah to be a prophet to the nations.

It's easy to forget that God puts that much foresight into the life of every believer. It's easy to see what's not going well and feel inadequate, or to question what God has in mind for my children when they fail. God prepared us with every trait we need for the work he has for us to do. Failure does not deter him. He knows how to overcome. Our weakness doesn't eliminate us from service either. His power is more than adequate to compensate for it.

God prepared us with every trait we need for the work he has for us to do.

Jeremiah wasn't convinced he would make a good prophet and proposed that God reconsider. God told Jeremiah that reconsidering wasn't part of his plan.

So Jeremiah began his ministry. But then it got

hard. Halfway through the book, Jeremiah told God off. He had been doing all God asked of him, and all he could see was the fun he wasn't having. Jeremiah told God:

"Think of how I suffer reproach for your sake. When your words came, I ate them; they were my joy and my heart's delight, for I bear your name, Lord God Almighty. I never sat in the company of revelers, never made merry with them; I sat alone because your hand was on me and you had filled me with indignation. Why is my pain unending and my wound grievous and incurable? You are to me like a deceptive brook, like a spring that fails" (Jeremiah 15:15-18).

In essence, Jeremiah told God ministry wasn't worth it.

You don't have to be a Christian long to succumb to the temptation to compare heavenly treasure with worldly gain. The time, money, and energy invested in kingdom work don't necessarily result in "more" here. It usually doesn't make for a hefty bank account or worldly status, and, in fact, often the only noticeable results are stress, fatigue, and the nagging feeling that you're not doing the task at hand justice.

That doesn't mean kingdom work is irrelevant or unworthy of your efforts. Far from it!

God told Jeremiah: **"'If you repent, I will restore you that you may serve me; if you utter** worthy, not worthless, words, you will be my spokesman. Let this people turn to you, but you must not turn to them. I will make you a wall to this people, a fortified wall of bronze; they will fight against you but will not overcome you, for I am with you to rescue and save you,' declares the Lord" (15:19,20).

God told Jeremiah to get a hold of his tongue because there was hard work ahead! The same message is ours. Kingdom work is hard, but complaining is not the answer. God is with us. Those who come against us will answer to him.

Kingdom work is hard, but complaining is not the answer.

The comfort of that concept often escapes me. I expect outsiders and unbelievers to rage against me. But when fellow Christians challenge motives, criticize methods, overlook me, refuse to hear me, gossip about me, put me down, label and laugh at me, I forget who's got my back.

The God of angel armies searches hearts and stands beside his faithful servants. He was good enough to show us as much in 2 Kings chapter 6. In this section of Scripture, the prophet Elisha and his servant were being hunted down by an enemy king. The king planned to capture Elisha, because Elisha was preventing him from successfully attacking Israel. We're told:

"When the servant of the man of God got up and went out early the next morning, an army with horses and chariots had surrounded the city. 'Oh no, my lord! What shall we do?' the servant asked. 'Don't be afraid,' the prophet answered. 'Those who are with us are more than those who are with them.' And Elisha prayed, 'Open his eyes, Lord, so that he may see.' Then the Lord opened the servant's eyes, and he looked and saw the hills full of horses and chariots of fire all around Elisha" (verses 15-17).

God sent an army of angels to defend his prophet. Even when we don't see, they are there defending us too. Pity the person who goes against God's workers serving in righteousness.

And when the servants of God falter in their duties, God will rebuke them as he rebuked Jeremiah, that they may be effective in their work.

Jeremiah's life and work were difficult. Jeremiah continued to speak God's Word, even when it was not what the people wanted to hear. Because he stood for the truth, his scrolls were burned by the king, he was beaten and put in prison, thrown in a cistern, kept under guard, ridiculed, starved, and sought, though his advice was never followed.

We, like Jeremiah, can start to feel our efforts to turn people to God are futile. How easily we forget our job is to proclaim Christ and his salvation. The results are up to God. Only the Holy Spirit can create and sustain faith.

If we only saw the hardship Jeremiah endured, we might despair and decide kingdom work isn't worth the effort. But we would miss the best part.

Only the Holy Spirit can create and sustain faith.

In Jeremiah chapter 39, the Babylonian army came against Israel, set the palace on fire, and captured the people. And this is what we read about Jeremiah, the man who had been forsaken by his people:

"Now Nebuchadnezzar king of Babylon had given these orders about Jeremiah through Nebuzaradan commander of the imperial guard: 'Take him and look after him; don't harm him but do for him whatever he asks.' So Nebuzaradan the commander of the guard, Nebushazban a chief officer, Nergal-Sharezer a high official and all the other officers of the king of Babylon sent and had Jeremiah taken out of the courtyard of the guard. They turned him over to Gedaliah . . . to take him back to his home. So he remained among his own people" (verses 11-14).

When Nebuchadnezzar, king of the known world at that time, captured Israel, he knew Jeremiah by name and made sure he was cared for. Nebuchadnezzar knew Jeremiah because God knew Jeremiah. And while everyone else was carried into captivity,

Jeremiah was able to stay in his homeland.

If you are feeling neglected and unappreciated, it's only because you aren't able to see God singing over you with delight. You don't see Jesus interceding on your behalf. Your mortal eyes can't see the Spirit breathing life into your weary soul.

Continue to fight the good fight. As you wait for deliverance, embrace the ways God is shaping you and growing your faith and trust in him. You may never have a Nebuchadnezzar moment on earth, where you alone are spared judgment and instead find favor. But when you reach the throne of God, your perseverance will be rewarded.

More to Think About

1. Most people who have been part of a church, or even the church at large, have experienced hurt. Something happened between church members or between yourself and your pastor or in your family. Are you hanging on to hurt from ministry that went wrong? Write down a few key words about that situation.

2. Read these words the apostle Paul wrote in 2 Timothy 16-18: **"At my first defense, no one came to my support, but everyone deserted me. May it not be held against them. But the Lord stood at my side and gave me strength, so that through me the message might be fully proclaimed and all the Gentiles might hear it. And I was delivered from the lion's mouth. The Lord will rescue me from every evil attack and will bring me safely to his heavenly kingdom. To him be glory for ever and ever. Amen."** What does this passage move you to do? How does it motivate you going forward?

Holy Father, the apostle Paul held nothing against those who deserted him. Help me forgive those who have hurt me. Where bitterness has crept into my heart, remove it completely. Redeem and restore what was taken away and put me where I can best serve you. Bless my ministry efforts to your glory. Precious Jesus, in your name I pray. Amen.

Esther:
She Didn't Ask for This Job

In the Old Testament book of Esther, we learn that a Jewish girl was orphaned and raised by her cousin Mordecai. Mordecai called her Hadassah. We know and refer to her by her Persian name, Esther.

As a young woman, she likely knew of the lavish banquet King Xerxes gave, since all the people of her citadel were invited. Surely she heard that King Xerxes banished Queen Vashti after the banquet. But could she imagine the fallout would have an impact on her?

Three to five years passed. Xerxes suffered major military losses. He returned home forlorn and without a queen. His advisors came up with a plan to cheer him. All the young beautiful virgins in the land were to be confiscated and "tried out" by King Xerxes. One by one they would be presented to him in the evening. The next morning they would return to his harem. From there, they would be at the mercy of his whims.

That Xerxes agreed to such a plan gives insight into his character. Arrogance and entitlement overshadowed any thought of taking girls from their families to be used or neglected. Any hope the girls had for marriage rested on the miniscule chance that they were the one chosen to be queen. All the others would be confined to the harem.

We may have no concept of harem life, but the "lost in his harem" feeling is easy to relate to. It is the experience of being stuck: in a job and unable to get an interview elsewhere, unemployed and overlooked, single and searching, suddenly divorced, stranded in

Who hasn't felt stuck at some point in his or her life?

the house with crabby kids, sick and unable to do the things you wish you could do. Who hasn't felt stuck at some point in his or her life?

The book of Genesis introduces us to Joseph. As a teenager he was sold into slavery by his jealous brothers. Though he served his master well, he was framed and put in prison through no wrongdoing of his own. Joseph begged another inmate, the king's official, to remember him when he returned to his royal position. Instead, the official forgot about him for two years.

It's hard to hang on to hope. It's much easier to sink into the despair of being forgotten. But God hadn't forgotten Joseph. He would go from prisoner to high government official in due time. Esther wasn't lost in the harem either. She was chosen, out of all the other young ladies, to be Xerxes' wife.

Certainly there were perks to being queen.

She lived in the palace with servants and beautiful clothes and jewelry. But her husband had a harem and was inaccessible to Esther except when he desired to be with her.

And then Mordecai showed up. Esther's beloved cousin refused to come to her but stayed outside the palace in sackcloth. He sent messages telling Esther the Jews were in trouble. Everyone she knew and loved would be subject to annihilation. He urged her to act. Even though it was against the law to go to the king without being summoned, he told her to go to her husband and plead for mercy for the Jews. She needed to stop Haman, the man plotting the evil against the Jews, the man who convinced Xerxes the world would be better without the Jews in it.

Have you been put on the spot with people looking at you to solve the issue at hand?

Have you been put on the spot with people looking at you to solve the issue at hand?

There's no women's Bible study at church. Would you start one?

Could you lead the building committee?

Would you consider speaking to this group, starting a mission society, joining the evangelism team, leading the Sunday school?

Like Esther you may find yourself digging in

your heals: *I didn't ask for this. I don't know what I'm doing. This could go badly.*

Generations of people used by God to do his will have felt the same. When the angel of the Lord came to Gideon with a calling to save Israel from the hands of the heathen nation ruling them at the time, the angel greeted Gideon with, **"The Lord is with you, mighty warrior"** (Judges 6:12). Gideon challenged both notions: God surely wasn't with him or Israel. If God were with Israel, they wouldn't be enslaved to the Midianites. And *warrior* would be the last word Gideon would use to describe himself. He was from the weakest clan and the smallest family.

And remember Moses, the man called to lead Israel from Egypt to the Promised Land and the 40 years in between? Moses told God to find someone else. He was not a good speaker. How could he lead Israel?

The Old Testament prophet Jeremiah excused himself from service because he was too young. Another Old Testament prophet, Isaiah, told God his uncouth language disqualified him.

Are you too old or uneducated? Are you shy or too outspoken? Do the sins of your past keep you from service?

Esther faced death for going to the king without his request. And if that wasn't enough, it had been 30 days since the king had asked for her.

What power did she yield? How could she leverage the king's actions or opinions when he hadn't thought of her for a month?

The devil is brilliant at convincing us that we yield no power. *Who are you? What talent do you claim? Why would anyone follow or listen to what you say? You're out of your league. Sit down, keep your mouth shut, and no one will get hurt.*

Thank God for the Mordecais of the world. Mordecai was unyielding in his push for Esther to be involved. **"If you remain silent at this time, relief and deliverance for the Jews will arise from another place, but you and your father's family will perish. And who knows but that you have come to royal position for such a time as this?"** (Esther 4:14).

Mordecai challenged Esther to consider why she was there. "Do you think, Esther, that God put you in the palace to eat fancy food? He put you here for his purposes and plans that you might be in a position to save his people!"

Why are you where you are? God's plan is never that we serve ourselves but that our lives are used to serve him and others. So you feel inadequate. Who doesn't? Do you feel unprepared? Then surely you will need God to guide you. Have your sins been great? Who better to share the freeing grace that lifts the burden of condemnation than you?

God has no pool of perfect candidates to

choose from. He has only flawed mortals to do the work. And God is undeterred.

God told the apostle Paul that his power is made perfect in weakness (2 Corinthians 12:9). God's power shines all the brighter through our inability. As mountains move, we can be sure it wasn't our greatness but God's at work.

How else could a speck of a man like Gideon destroy a mighty army with a trumpet and a jar? And how could a man like Moses with very little charisma lead millions of people for 40 years? And how could Isaiah, a man of unclean tongue, write some of the most quoted poetic prophecy? And how did Joseph go from being the despised brother who was sold to get him out of his older brothers' sight to the second-highest position in the land? How, but for the grace of God, did Esther, a forgotten wife, gather the courage to stand before the most powerful man of the land, unsummoned and against the law, to ask him to lunch and ultimately to save her people?

They did these things the exact way you will. Clothed in power from on high and wrapped in courage only God could give, they did what seemed unthinkable, not just to them but to everyone else as well.

If you are called to a ministry you wouldn't have chosen and feel inadequate to do what's needed, you're in good company. Take heart! If

God has called you to it, he will help you through it in amazing and miraculous ways.

More to Think About

1. Esther spent three days fasting and praying before she went to see the king unsummoned. Her maids and all the Jewish people prayed with her and for her. When I was asked to lead a Bible study I felt unqualified to teach, I asked all the members of the adult spiritual growth team at my church to hold me in prayer prior to the first class. My prayers were for God to give me all the qualities I needed to teach well. Esther and the Jews likely prayed for Esther to find favor with her husband so she would get the opportunity to speak to him on the Jews' behalf. What work have you been asked to do or what area of ministry would you love to do if you were able?

2. List the talents or characteristics you would need to do that ministry well.

3. Now pray for God to grant you those qualities in generous portion to do the work for his glory. Ask your closest friends to pray the same.

Heavenly Father, the harvest is great, but the workers are few. Call and equip your servants to serve in the harvest field. Help us be like Mordecai to spur the timid. Remind all who struggle with feelings of inadequacy that you are the strength and the force and the power we need. We go at Jesus' request and in Jesus' name. Amen.

Peter:
A Work in Progress

Peter, also called Simon or Simon Peter, is the guy for those of us who are passionately in love with the Lord but stumble around a bit before getting ministry right.

Five of the twelve disciples are only mentioned by name in the Bible. Of the remaining seven, Andrew is only talked about a few times, and Thomas and Philip are spoken of in brief accounts. Peter was one of the three disciples who comprised Jesus' inner circle, and, of the disciples, he was the one written about most. Peter was one of those larger-than-life, in the spotlight, always-has-something-to-say kind of guys.

No one would deny Peter's passion. The day Jesus called Peter into full-time ministry, Jesus got into Peter's boat to teach the crowd along the shore of the Sea of Galilee. When Jesus finished speaking, he told Peter, **"'Put out into deeper water, and let down the nets for a catch.' Simon answered, 'Master, we've worked hard all night and haven't caught anything. But because you say so, I will let down the nets.' When they had done so, they caught such a large number of fish that their nets began to break. So they signaled their partners in the other boat to come and help** them, and they came and filled both boats so full that they began to sink"** (Luke 5:4-7).

Luke's account tells us: **"When Simon Peter saw this, he fell at Jesus' knees and said, 'Go away from me, Lord; I am a sinful man!' For he and all his companions were astonished at the catch of fish they had taken"** (5:8,9).

In the presence of holiness, a grown man fell to the ground confessing his sinfulness. That's passion. It's the same passion that three years later caused him to jump out of a boat and into the water to run to shore after realizing Jesus, risen from the dead, was there to meet them (John 21).

Do you know someone who is quick to spring to action whenever and wherever needed, who isn't afraid to let people know the love of his or her Savior?

Long before David was the beloved king of Israel, he was a teenager with the job of tending his father's sheep.

Do you know someone who is quick to spring to action whenever and wherever needed?

One day his father, Jesse, sent him to the battlefield where his older brothers were stationed to find out how things were going. When David arrived, he heard the taunts of Goliath, a giant from the enemy camp.

David couldn't believe the way Goliath mocked

Israel. Without hesitation, he volunteered to fight Goliath. David's oldest brother called him wicked and conceited for thinking he could kill the giant.

But David's plan wasn't to go against Goliath using his own strength. When David went out to fight Goliath, he said, **"You come against me with sword and spear and javelin, but I come against you in the name of the Lord Almighty, the God of the armies of Israel, whom you have defied. This day the Lord will deliver you into my hands . . . and the whole world will know that there is a God in Israel. All those gathered here will know that it is not by sword or spear that the Lord saves; for the battle is the Lord's, and he will give all of you into our hands"** (1 Samuel 17:45-47).

Peter's passion was commendable, even admirable, but unlike David, Peter's courage sometimes failed. When the disciples were in the boat in the middle of the night and thought they saw a ghost walking toward them, Jesus identified himself and told them not to be afraid.

Peter responded, **"Lord, if it's you . . . tell me to come to you on the water"** (Matthew 14:28).

Jesus told him to come, so Peter sprung out of the boat and began walking on the water. But Peter lost his courage and began to sink. When Jesus pulled him up, he rebuked him, **"'You of little faith,' he said, 'why did you doubt?'"** (verse 31).

Peter's courage failed him again on the night

Jesus was captured in the Garden of Gethsemane. When Peter followed Jesus to the courtyard of the high priest, a servant girl asked if he had been with Jesus. He denied it emphatically. When others suggested he was one of Jesus' disciples, Peter called down curses in his denial (Mark 14:66-72).

Peter was a work in progress. The desire was there, but his faint heart betrayed him at times.

Peter was a work in progress. The desire was there, but his faint heart betrayed him at times.

John Mark, who would later be a valued companion of Peter, didn't have a great ministry start either. His first ministry experience was as a companion to Barnabas and Paul on their first missionary journey. When Paul and Barnabas were preparing for their second journey, we find out John Mark only made it through part of the first journey before turning back. Acts 15:37 reports, **"Barnabas wanted to take John, also called Mark, with them, but Paul did not think it wise to take him, because he had deserted them in Pamphylia and had not continued with them in the work."**

As wonderful as it would be if we all started our ministry journeys off with great success, some of us stumble. I bombed several situations early in my ministry. I wish I could say I handled every situation well and had no need to apologize even today. But while the many years I've held leadership positions have seasoned me to handle some things better than I would have 15 years ago, I will never have it all together.

Thankfully God doesn't have a problem using a work in progress. Initial failure doesn't need to define us. And failure from a worldly standpoint is not the be-all and end-all. The Sunday school teacher in a small town who passionately teaches the Word to five children is no less of a soldier in God's army than the pastor of a huge church, despite the world's value on numbers.

It is a comfort and blessing that God showed us Peter's weaknesses. God showed us Peter's propensity to opening his mouth before thinking and jumping into something with little thought of consequence. And he showed us how he can take a man like that and use him in mighty ways for his glory. He showed that with the help of the Spirit, the man who cowered in front of a servant girl and refused to acknowledge Jesus could later stand before a crowd of thousands professing Jesus as his Savior. And through Peter's letters, God showed he could take an impulsive man and teach him self-control.

It was Peter who wrote, **"Always be prepared to give an answer to everyone who asks you to give the reason for the hope that you have"**

(1 Peter 3:15). That's Peter's willingness to jump right in.

"But," he continues, **"do this with gentleness and respect, keeping a clear conscience, so that those who speak maliciously against your good behavior in Christ may be ashamed of their slander"** (verses 15,16). This was a more mature Peter who had learned self-control.

Maybe you know a young, passionate Christian. Maybe his or her enthusiasm without adequate thought drives you a little, or even a lot, crazy. Maybe your first instinct is to squash him or her and put that person in his or her place.

Before you do that, consider Peter. Jesus didn't squash his enthusiasm. He didn't respond to his silly suggestion to build a shelter for each of the men on the Mount of Transfiguration (Matthew 17:1-8). (Peter was forgetting that two of the men resided in heaven and that earth would not be Jesus' permanent residence either.) Jesus prayed for Peter (Luke 22:32), poured himself into Peter, and forgave Peter, giving him another opportunity even after he blew it big time (John 21). And over time Peter became a significant kingdom worker.

These days I pray my passion outweighs my folly. I'm grateful God's mercy led many to pour into me and guide and encourage me throughout the years. We all need to do the same with the next generation of rambunctious and passionate Christians.

More to Think About

1. For ministry to continue, younger people have to get involved and eventually take over the tasks. The person who takes over may or may not do ministry the way it was done before. What should we keep in mind when it comes to the younger generation and kingdom work?

2. Think of the people who have been foundational in your ministry (whether you are in public ministry or serving in some capacity in your church or trying to be a Christian in your community and/or home). What did those people do to get you into ministry, to encourage you while in ministry, or to come alongside you when ministry or life was hard?

3. Once you've identified ways you've been helped and nurtured, identify someone you can nurture and encourage too.

Lord, you see where we have stumbled. Put together what our folly has torn apart. Refine us so we can be used by you. Help us see those we can encourage and act on the Spirit's nudging. In Jesus' name. Amen.

The Woman at the Well: An Unlikely Missionary

John chapter 4 gives us a glimpse into the indiscriminating heart of God. The climate around Jerusalem was becoming hostile to Christ. Because his time to die was still years away, Jesus left Judea and traveled north several days to live once more in Galilee.

John tells us Jesus **"had to go through Samaria"** (4:4). "Had to" in that sentence is the same "had to" children use when telling their friends they "had to" do the dishes. Most Jews went out of their way to avoid Samaria. Jesus had to go there, not because it was the only or preferred way, but because he had a divine appointment with the last person on earth anyone would pick for ministry.

Jesus arrived at Jacob's Well at noon, the hottest part of the day. No one in their right mind would be getting water then; no one except a woman with a past and a present, a woman hoping to avoid those who would look down on her.

This is a good place for a heart check; a time to consider how we view others. Sitting at home in front of my Bible I may be godly enough, but give me a chance and I'll push past others to be first. I'll neglect the weak in my selfishness. I'll pray others are generous while clinging to my wallet. And I'm pretty sure if it was the right day, I could turn up my nose at a woman who has been in and out of five marriages, or a disheveled teen, or a man with a sloppy haircut.

Everything about Jesus contradicts this behavior. He habitually noticed the hurt, pursued the broken, and encouraged the weak.

A few men (Daniel, David, and Joseph come to mind) were uniquely qualified and gifted for ministry with a long list of skills. Most of the rest of those used by God throughout Scripture were flawed and/or scarred to the extent *they* thought they were unusable.

Would we have frowned at God's choice in Moses or Rahab or Samson? Would we have followed Gideon or listened to Isaiah?

While the disciples searched for food, Jesus overlooked exhaustion, hunger, and heat to talk with a woman few would notice.

Are we so willing to pour into others when it's inconvenient or hard? And can we overlook the hard surface and sometimes rude exterior that might turn others away?

One day a young boy knocked on our door. I would later come to find he was 8 years old and lived several blocks away. He had seen my 16-year-old son riding a motorbike around the neighborhood and followed him home. He unabashedly asked to see the boy with the motorbike.

It didn't take long to realize this boy needed Jesus. This chubby spitfire ran the neighborhood; talked like a sailor; and knew how to talk his way in, out, and around most situations.

The first time he ate at our house, he took several bites of his meal, pushed his plate aside, and said, "I've had better." (No lie!) My gracious husband assured him that at our house no one was forced to eat anything and what he didn't want the dog would gladly accept.

Jesus, in his omniscience, had to know it wasn't going to be easy with the woman at the well. She had been around, and there were plenty of scars to prove it. Right off the bat she wondered what business he had asking her to get him a drink. He was a Jew and she was a Samaritan. And he could forget about getting smart. The well was deep, and he had nothing to draw with, so there.

This woman didn't know Jesus or that she had a need for him. Lifelong Christians may know Jesus, but they aren't immune from losing the desire to follow him. They can fall into a "God, you need me" or "I'll take the lead" mentality.

Several kings in the Old Testament of the Bible started their reign well. They eagerly set about doing God's work, and in response God blessed them and gave them success. Then pride showed up, and it became more about them than God.

We fall into the same trap if we think because

we volunteer at a church or lead in some capacity or have held a role for a number of years that our voices should carry more weight than someone else's. It happens when we think the church should go the direction we think is best all the time. At that point we've lost the servant mentality that Jesus desires his disciples to have.

Jesus told his disciples and us: **"You know that the rulers of the Gentiles lord it over them, and their high officials exercise authority over them. Not so with you. Instead, whoever wants to become great among you must be your servant, and whoever wants to be first must be your slave—just as the Son of Man did not come to be served, but to serve, and to give his life as a ransom for many"** (Matthew 20:25-28).

It is not that God needs us. He wants us. He delights in using us for his glory in his kingdom, but not for us to become haughty.

God knows what it takes to call us and keep us close to him. Jesus, sitting at the well in Samaria, knew the woman's past.

It is not that God needs us. He wants us. He delights in using us for his glory.

That's why he told her to go get her husband.

"'I have no husband,' she replied. Jesus said to her, 'You are right when you say you have no husband. The fact is, you have had five hus-

bands, and the man you now have is not your husband. What you have just said is quite true'" (John 4:17,18).

It is breathtaking to realize God knows us in and out. He knows our hurts, our fears, our worries, and our weaknesses. He knows where we've stumbled and where we like to hide.

David, the shepherd who became the first king of Israel, said it best in Psalm 139:1-6: **"You have searched me, Lord, and you know me. You know when I sit and when I rise; you perceive my thoughts from afar. You discern my going out and my lying down; you are familiar with all my ways. Before a word is on my tongue you, Lord, know it completely. You hem me in behind and before, and you lay your hand upon me. Such knowledge is too wonderful for me, too lofty for me to attain."**

The woman at the well realized Jesus was not like anyone else she had ever met. And when he told her he was the Messiah, she left her water jar at that well and ran to tell everyone she knew. Everyone. Even those who looked down on her.

We're told: **"Many of the Samaritans from that town believed in him because of the woman's testimony"** (John 4:39).

One woman who knew the truth brought a town to know their Savior. What could you do?

God has heard all the reasons you can't do it,

but let's cross off "unsavory past." When you meet Jesus and turn in true repentance from your sin, it is forgiven. King David said in Psalm 103:12: **"As far as the east is from the west, so far has he removed our transgressions from us."**

God doesn't just push our sin aside to remember it another day. He banishes it. The blood of Christ removes it. Satan is good at dredging it up to accuse us and hold it against us, but not God.

Simon Peter betrayed Jesus by denying any association with him. After Jesus rose from the dead, Peter was one of the first people Jesus appeared to. Later he met Peter on the shore of Galilee and reinstated him for service. No doubt Peter thought his sin disqualified him. But

God doesn't push our sin aside to remember it another day. He banishes it.

Jesus sought Peter, talked and walked with him, and commissioned him to take care of the people of God after Jesus ascended into heaven.

Another disciple, Thomas, refused to believe Jesus had risen from the dead. Jesus came back and showed himself to Thomas.

Jesus' half brother James didn't believe in Jesus until after he rose from the dead. Jesus didn't hold it against him or consider it a disqualification. James worked in the church and wrote the book by his name.

Our past sins do not make us ineligible. God can and will use willing hearts, indiscriminately, for his glory.

More to Think About

1. Have you ever felt like something you've done disqualifies you from serving God in any useful way? Why do you feel that way?

2. What does the story of the woman at the well tell you about your sin and usefulness?

Holy Father, you know every part of me.
You know where I belong. You created me to
do your work. Show me what you would have me
do. Help me see the cues. Use my weaknesses
to glorify you. Help me, Jesus. Amen.

Conclusion

When it comes to ministry and being a light in a dark world, keep trying even if you don't know what you're doing and even if you get it wrong at first. Persevere even when you wonder if what you do makes a difference. Do what God leads you to even if you're scared. Stay passionate, and pray that self-control kicks in. Don't let your scars deter you. Let God use them in mighty ways **". . . being confident of this, that he who began a good work in you will carry it on to completion until the day of Christ Jesus"** (Philippians 1:6).

About the Writer

Amber Albee Swenson has authored several books: *Borderline: Drawing the Line at Those Seven "Little" Deadly Sins in Today's Culture of Compromise; Bible Moms; The Whisper Theory* and its sequel, *The Bread of Angels*; and *Ladies of Legacy*. She is a regular blogger for Time of Grace. She also writes an occasional devotional blog and is a regular contributor to several Christian organizations. In 2011 she started speaking to women with the intent of bringing the Bible to life in tangible, applicable ways. Speaking has taken her and her eager-to-travel family to places they likely would not have found on their own. Amber's husband and four children keep life exciting and give her lots to write and pray about. Mostly she's amazed at God's goodness, awed by his wisdom and desire to grow her, and continually stretched by his calling in her life.

About Time of Grace

Time of Grace is for people who want more growth and less struggle in their spiritual walk. The timeless truth of God's Word is delivered through television, print, and digital media with millions of content engagements each month. We connect people to God's grace so they know they are loved and forgiven and so they can start living in the freedom they've always wanted. To discover more, please visit timeofgrace.org, download our free app at timeofgrace.org/app, or call 800.661.3311.

Help share God's message of grace!

Every gift you give helps Time of Grace reach people around the world with the good news of Jesus. Your generosity and prayer support take the gospel of grace to others through our ministry outreach and help them find the restart with Jesus they need.

Give today at timeofgrace.org/give or by calling 800.661.3311.

Thank you!